ALASKA

A Picture Book to Remember Her by

CRESCENT BOOKS
NEW YORK

CLB 1702
© 1987 Illustrations and text: Colour Library Books Ltd.,
Guildford, Surrey, England.
Text filmsetting by Acesetters Ltd., Richmond, Surrey, England.
All rights reserved.
Printed and bound in Barcelona. Spain by Cronion, S.A.
1987 edition published by Crescent Books, distributed by Crown Publishers, Inc.
ISBN 0 517 62359 5
h g f e d c b a

It's entirely appropriate that Alaska was one of the last two states admitted to the Union. More than any other it is still a place where a family can lead a life similar to the pioneers who expanded the country westward. And more than any other, there is more future there than past.

Almost 90 percent of the 438,000 people who live in its nearly 587,000 square miles either came from one of the other states or have parents who did, but few have any intention of going back. By and large they like it there, where the wilderness is at your back door and the idea of "rugged individualism" is a necessary way of life.

It's a place of spectacular scenery that includes North America's highest mountain, its biggest glaciers, the greatest untouched wilderness anywhere in the United States.

It's a place that was largely left untouched by the government after it was bought from Russia for $7.2 million in 1867. It wasn't until 1903 that a Congressional committee was formed to have a legislative look at the place, and their findings didn't go far beyond the discovery that there wasn't a single road a wagon could use anywhere in the territory. It took them ten more years to do anything about it and then all they did was build a 370-mile dirt road from Valdez on the coast to Fairbanks in the interior.

Things got better during World War II, when the territory was considered strategic and roads vital to the war effort, but the government went to sleep again until the late 1950s when Alaska was grudgingly included in the Federal Highway Program. The result is that the roads in Alaska aren't as good or as extensive as in any other state. The result of that is that most Alaskans live in communities, but not many of their towns are connected together. Except by air. Alaskans use airplanes almost as much as their fellow Americans use automobiles. It's the only way to get around the vast territory, they say. But just as important, the freedom of flight appeals to their pioneering spirit, the same spirit that sets them apart from their neighbors to the south.

Because a huge part of the state lies north of the Arctic Circle and because it is a land dotted with glaciers and snow-capped mountains, most Americans think of Alaska as a place where you never shed your woollies. The fact is that along the Pacific coast, the climate is very much like New England, except the winters are a bit warmer. Up in the Yukon, the territory Jack London told us about, the winter temperatures drop 40 or 50 degrees below zero Fahrenheit, but as any sourdough up in Nome will tell you, there is no wind. And it could be worse. Fort Yukon has recorded temperatures as low as 78 degrees below zero in January. That same year, the mercury went up to 100 in June.

Previous page: the Delta River region of the Alaska Range.

Facing page: a moose.

Above: Juneau, capital city of Alaska. Right and far right: some of the spectacular scenery to be seen along the Inland Passage. Below: the town of Petersburg on Kupreanof Island.

Originally known as Harrisburg, Juneau (these pages) was founded in 1900 by two gold prospectors, Dick Harris and Joe Juneau.

Facing page: the lower slopes of Mount Juneau. Remaining pictures: Juneau. Overleaf: (left) Juneau Marina and (right) Auke Bay.

Top left: float planes near Juneau. Top right, above and left: Glacier Bay National Park. Far left: the Mendenhall Glacier.

Encompassing far more territory than the inlet for which it is named, Glacier Bay National Park (these pages) has many attractions. Overleaf: (top left) a small port; (bottom left) houses near Valdez and (right) Mineral Creek, near Valdez.

Left: Mount Drum, in the Wrangell Mountains, overshadows the airport at Gulkana. Above: a snowmobile and (top) its predecessor, the husky.

The caribou (left and bottom right) differs from other deer in that both sexes sport antlers. Below: a trapper's derelict cabin slowly collapsing into its surroundings. Bottom left: the Black Rapids in the Delta River area.

Below: a caribou, the most prolific deer in Alaska. Right and far right: sections of the famous 800-mile-long pipeline which carries oil across Alaska from the Prudhoe Bay field southward to the Valdez terminal. Signboards (bottom left and bottom right) tell visitors much about the pipeline, problems concerning its construction, and the wildlife of the region.

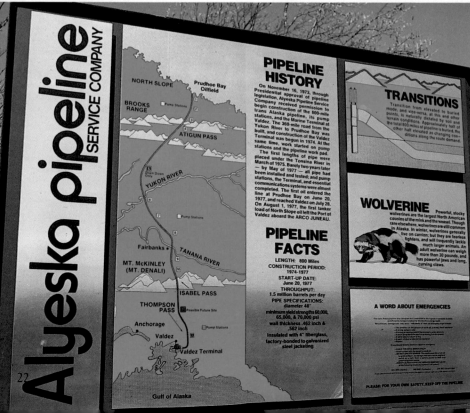

Alyeska pipeline SERVICE COMPANY

NORTH SLOPE
Prudhoe Bay Oilfield

BROOKS RANGE

Pump Stations

ATIGUN PASS

YUKON RIVER

Pump Stations

Fairbanks

MT. McKINLEY (MT. DENALI)

TANANA RIVER

ISABEL PASS

THOMPSON PASS

Possible Future Site

Anchorage

Valdez

Pump Stations

Valdez Terminal

Gulf of Alaska

PIPELINE HISTORY

On November 16, 1973, through Presidential approval of pipeline legislation, Alyeska Pipeline Service Company received permission to begin construction of the 800-mile trans Alaska pipeline, its pump stations, and the Marine Terminal at Valdez. The 360-mile road from the Yukon River to Prudhoe Bay was built, and construction of the Valdez Terminal was begun in 1974. At the same time, work started on pump stations and the pipeline work pad.

The first lengths of pipe were placed under the Tonsina River in March of 1975. Barely two years later — by May of 1977 — all pipe had been installed and tested, and pump stations, the Terminal, and essential communications systems were almost completed. The first oil entered the line at Prudhoe Bay on June 20, 1977, and reached Valdez on July 28. On August 1, 1977, the first tanker load of North Slope oil left the Port of Valdez aboard the ARCO JUNEAU.

PIPELINE FACTS

LENGTH: 800 Miles
CONSTRUCTION PERIOD: 1974-1977
START-UP DATE: June 20, 1977
THROUGHPUT: 1.5 million barrels per day
PIPE SPECIFICATIONS: diameter 48"
minimum yield strengths 60,000, 65,000, & 70,000 psi
wall thickness .462 inch & .562 inch
insulated with 4" fiberglass, factory-bonded to galvanized steel jacketing

TRANSITIONS

Transition from elevated to buried mode, and vice-versa, at this and other points, is naturally dictated by soil and terrain conditions. Approximately half of the total 800 miles of pipeline is buried, the other half elevated as changing conditions along the route demand.

WOLVERINE

Powerful, stocky wolverines are the largest North American cousins of the mink and the weasel. Though rare elsewhere, wolverines are still common in Alaska. In winter, wolverines generally live on carrion; but they are fearless fighters, and will frequently tackle much larger animals. An adult wolverine can weigh more than 30 pounds, and has powerful jaws and long, curving claws.

A WORD ABOUT EMERGENCIES

PLEASE: FOR YOUR OWN SAFETY, KEEP OFF THE PIPELINE.

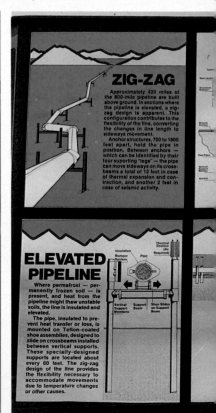

ZIG-ZAG

Approximately 420 miles of the 800-mile pipeline are built above ground. In sections where the pipeline is elevated, a zig-zag design is apparent. This configuration contributes to the flexibility of the line, converting the changes in line length to sideways movement.

Anchor structures, 700 to 1800 feet apart, hold the pipe in position. Between anchors — which can be identified by their four suporting "legs" — the pipe can move sideways on its crossbeams a total of 12 feet in case of thermal expansion and contraction, and another 2 feet in case of seismic activity.

ELEVATED PIPELINE

Where permafrost — permanently frozen soil — is present, and heat from the pipeline might thaw unstable soils, the line is insulated and elevated.

The pipe, insulated to prevent heat transfer or loss, is mounted on Teflon-coated shoe assemblies, designed to slide on crossbeams installed between vertical supports. These specially-designed supports are located about every 60 feet. The zig-zag design of the line provides the flexibility necessary to accommodate movements due to temperature changes or other causes.

HEAT PIPES

In areas where the frozen-soil temperatures are near the thaw point, heat pipes are installed inside the pipeline's vertical supports. The finned radiators above the supports are the external extensions of these heat pipes, which employ a fluid with a low boiling point to take heat from the ground through vaporization and condensation.

Heat from the soil enters the lower end of a sealed tube, causing the fluid inside to boil. The resulting vapor rises to the radiator and condenses, releasing energy. The condensate then returns to the bottom of the tube, as a film along the tube wall.

BURIED ROAD CROSSING

...points along the pipeline where ...ct its route, the line is buried. ..., conventional burial methods ... stable soils, with the pipe ... deep ditch and insulated with ...ng and dirt fill. Where thaw-...s are present, as they are ... is buried and special "heat ...nserted into the ground to ...and prevent thawing.

23

Panning for gold (left, above and top), near
Fairbanks, has changed little since the early days
of the gold rush, though the dredging machine
(inset top left) indicates the more mechanized
side of the business. Overleaf: (left) forests
near Fairbanks and (right) Denali National Park.

Right: Fairbanks, on the banks of the Chena River.
Above: a roadside hotel and restaurant at Ester.
Center: the historic theme park of Alaskaland. Top: the
sternwheeler *Discovery II* on the Tanana River.

Denali National Park (these pages and overleaf) is home to caribou (below) and the Toklat grizzly bear (above and right) as well as the setting for spectacular scenery: (facing page) the Susitna River; (overleaf left) Mount McKinley and (overleaf right) the Ruth Glacier.

City of startling contrasts, Anchorage, with its gleaming high-rise office developments (far left) and more typical low buildings (top), enjoys a spectacular setting on Cook Inlet with the rugged mountains as a backdrop. Top: 4th Avenue. Above: the helicopter section of Anchorage International Airport. Left: William Egan Civic and Convention Center.

Anchorage. Far left: Anchorage International Airport. Below: a sign outside the Visitor Information Center. Overleaf: (top left, center left and bottom left) Lake Hood, which claims to be the world's largest floatplane airport, and (right) city suburbs.

Left: five locomotives haul a long goods train through Moose Pass. Below: a lake in the Portage Glacier region. Bottom left: Seward Boat Harbor. Bottom right: Turnagain Arm, near Portage.

Top: fishing in the waters of Turnagain Arm. Center: a frozen lake near Portage. Above: a scene beside the Seward Highway. Right: boat harbor at Portage.

Facing page: (top) the Portage Glacier and (bottom) the Portage River. Top: Seward. Above and left: fishing in Turnagain Arm. Overleaf: a nearby tidewater glacier.

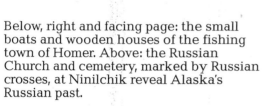

Below, right and facing page: the small boats and wooden houses of the fishing town of Homer. Above: the Russian Church and cemetery, marked by Russian crosses, at Ninilchik reveal Alaska's Russian past.

Left, top and center: the fishermen of Homer land their rich catches. Above: brightly painted Indian "spirit houses" and the Russian Orthodox church at Eklutna.

51

The traditional form of transport around Alaska, the husky sled, is tested to the full in the 1,049-mile Iditarod Race (these pages).

Travelling across the
frozen Alaskan landscape,
the competitors in the
Iditarod race face one of
the sternest tests of
endurance in existence and
have to be extensively
equiped for survival.
Overleaf left: a snow-
covered home in McGrath on
the Kuskokwim River.

55

The entrants in the Iditarod and locals (this page) are a varied group of people whose common bond is their independence. Facing page: a sled crossing the frozen Norton Sound.

Above: clutter surrounds an Eskimo home in Nome. Left: a more major thoroughfare in the town. Top: children play on a motorized tricycle in Kotzebue.

Some 30 miles south of the Arctic Circle, on the shores of the Bering Sea, Nome (below) is an old gold-mining town which has preserved many relics of its past. Facing page: the frozen Barents Sea. Overleaf: a scene near Iditarod.